KINDNESS

by Jane Belk Moncure
illustrated by Linda Sommers Hohag

THE CHILD'S WORLD

ELGIN, ILLINOIS 60120

Distributed by Childrens Press, 1224 West Van Buren Street, Chicago, Illinois 60607.

Library of Congress Cataloging in Publication Data

Moncure, Jane Belk.
  Kindness.

  (What is it?)
  SUMMARY: Explores the nature of kindness.
  1. Kindness—Addresses, essays, lectures.
(1. Kindness) I. Hohag, Linda. II. Title
BJ1533.K5M58   1981   177′.7   80-39535
ISBN 0-89565-204-8

KINDNESS

What is kindness?

Kindness is making a card for a friend
who has the chicken pox.

When my sister jumps out of the
waves, all shivery wet, and I give her
my towel, that's kindness.

Kindness is holding the umbrella
mostly over the other person when
we walk in the rain.

Kindness is helping my grandfather
rake leaves, even when no one asks
me to do it.

Kindness is buttoning up a sweater
for someone who hasn't learned how
to button yet.

Kindness is tying a shoe, so my sister will
not trip on the string.

Kindness is being gentle when I play
with my puppy,

or pick up a frog,

or hold a grasshopper in my hand.

Kindness is making a surprise birthday
cake for Mom,

or bringing Dad a glass of lemonade
when he is hot.

When a friend forgets his lunch box,
kindness is giving him one of my
sandwiches.

When a friend gets mad at you just
because he's tired and grumpy, then says
he's sorry, kindness is saying, "That's
O.K. I get mad sometimes too."

Kindness is giving my friend part of
my ice cream, because she dropped
hers on the ground.

Kindness is giving someone a turn to
swing in my swing,

or to slide down my slide,

or to sit in my wagon and take a ride.

When a friend breaks your model
airplane and then wants a piece of your
bubble gum, and you give it to him—
that's kindness.

Saying "Thank you" to your teacher
when she tells a story you like, that's
kindness.

Kindness is being friendly to a new
girl at school.

Kindness is holding a door open for
someone whose arms are full.

Kindness is helping put the books
back on the shelf.

Kindness brings happiness to others.

Can you think of other ways to
show kindness?

About the Author:

Jane Belk Moncure, author of many books and stories for young children, is a graduate of Virginia Commonwealth University and Columbia University. She has taught nursery, kindergarten and primary children in Europe and America. Mrs. Moncure has taught early childhood education while serving on the faculties of Virginia Commonwealth University and the University of Richmond. She was the first president of the Virginia Association for Early Childhood Education and has been recognized widely for her services to young children. She is married to Dr. James A. Moncure, Vice President of Elon College, and currently lives in Burlington, North Carolina.

About the Artist:

Linda Hohag is a graduate of the Cleveland Institute of Art in Cleveland, Ohio. She worked for the American Greeting Corporation in Cleveland, Ohio, for several years; and for the past seven years she has worked as a freelance artist. In addition to illustrating many, many books for children, Mrs. Hohag has designed products for the Toystalgia Company and the Stancraft Corporation. Mrs. Hohag says her favorite kind of work is illustrating children's books.